D1567992

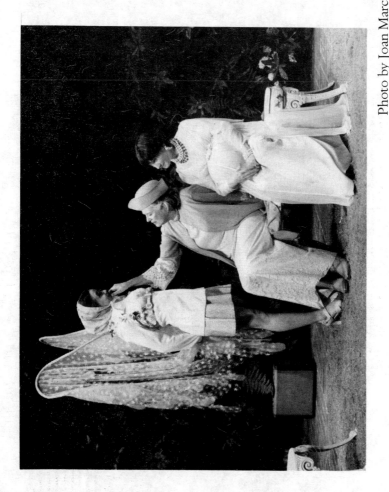

A scene from the Roundabout Theatre Company production of *Impossible Marriage*. Set design by Thomas Lynch.

Photo by Joan Marcus

IMPOSSIBLE MARRIAGE

BY
BETH HENLEY

★

DRAMATISTS
PLAY SERVICE
INC.

Dedicated to Patrick,
whom I love an impossible lot.
Forever and ever.

IMPOSSIBLE MARRIAGE was produced by Roundabout Theatre Company (Todd Haimes, Artistic Director; Ellen Richard, General Manager) in New York City in October 1998. It was directed by Stephen Wadsworth; the set design was by Thomas Lynch; the costume design was by Martin Pakledinaz; the lighting design was by Peter Kaczorowski; the sound design was by Dan Wojnar; and the production stage manager was Jay Adler. The cast was as follows:

SIDNEY LUNT .... Daniel London
FLORAL WHITMAN .... Holly Hunter
KANDALL KINGSLEY .... Lois Smith
JONSEY WHITMAN .... Jon Tenney
PANDORA KINGSLEY .... Gretchen Cleevely
REVEREND JONATHAN LARENCE .... Alan Mandell
EDVARD LUNT .... Christopher McCann

THE CAST
(In Order of Appearance)

SIDNEY LUNT
20s, son of the groom

FLORAL WHITMAN
30, older sister of the bride

KANDALL KINGSLEY
50s, mother of the bride

JONSEY WHITMAN
30s, brother-in-law of the bride, married to Floral

PANDORA KINGSLEY
20, the bride

REVEREND JONATHAN LARENCE
20s-50s, the reverend

EDVARD LUNT
50s, the groom

THE SETTING

The entire play takes place in Kandall Kingsley's garden on her country estate somewhere outside of Savannah.

The garden has many entrances and exits: some leading to the manor; some into the woods.

THE TIME

Mid-May

The play is performed without intermission.

IMPOSSIBLE MARRIAGE

PART ONE

A young man, Sidney, with a beard and wire glasses, enters. He carries a stick and walks across the stage rather menacingly, as he talks to himself and the gods. He stops, looks at a row of flowers, wacks them with his cane, laughs, reflects, twirls his cane, and exits. Floral, 30, enters from the manor. She is dressed in lace, acutely pregnant and severely distraught.

FLORAL. How will it end? *(Floral unbuttons the top button of her blouse, fans herself with a handkerchief, mops her forehead with it, looks down at her belly, moves around in a circle and sits down on a bench. She rocks and sings a song to soothe herself, something like "I'm Young And Healthy."* Kandall, 50s, a beautiful, elegantly coiffed woman, enters from the manor.)*

KANDALL. Why must you run off and cry?

FLORAL. I'm not crying.

KANDALL. You knocked over the Reverend's tea.

FLORAL. I did not.

KANDALL. What is it, Floral? What has upset you?

FLORAL. Nothing, Mother. Please.

KANDALL. Tell me, darling.

FLORAL. I swept up all these leaves and no one noticed. No one thanked me. I do my best to help, but nothing I do makes an impression. They're all ungrateful.

KANDALL. It's a good job. Yes. You've done a very good job with the leaves, but you shouldn't be lifting rakes.

FLORAL. Now you turn on me. *(Jonsey, 30s, an almost embarrassingly handsome man, enters from the manor.)*

JONSEY. *(To Floral.)* There you are, dearest. Why did you run

*See Special Note on Songs and Recordings on copyright page.

7

off? Were you crying?

FLORAL. No.

KANDALL. The leaves, she raked them up. You should be ashamed letting your wife, in her condition, lift and tote like a day laborer. I'm surprised at you, Jonsey. You ought to have more sense.

FLORAL. Don't blame him. He doesn't know any better.

JONSEY. I apologize to everyone. Forgive me, forgive me. There now, it's settled. It's all settled. Here, I've brought you some chocolate wrapped in gold. *(He hands them to Floral.)* She eats all the time. She has such cravings. Now about these leaves, I'll sweep them up.

FLORAL. *(Eating chocolate.)* I've done them all. They're raked. No one else thought of it but me. The wedding's tomorrow and I'm the only one who considered the leaves.

KANDALL. Have we heard anything further from the groom?

JONSEY. No word, I'm afraid.

FLORAL. He's probably not coming, the dog. I kill myself over these leaves and he leaves her screaming at the altar.

KANDALL. Don't be melodramatic. He's coming. I'm sure he's coming.

FLORAL. What makes you sure?

KANDALL. It's such a very bad match.

FLORAL. You'll get no arguments there. And, I am forced to say, Reverend Larence is a ridiculous looking man. I had to restrain myself from patting him for luck on the head like a hunchback.

KANDALL. Don't be wicked. I don't like you when you're wicked.

FLORAL. You'd like me if I stopped this wedding.

KANDALL. How would you do that?

FLORAL. Wickedly.

JONSEY. They're coming. The Reverend, Pandora. Sssh. *(From the manor, Pandora, 20, the image of youthful exuberance, enters with Reverend Jonathan Larence, a strange looking man with an innocent aura that can be alternately interpreted as idiotic and wise.)*

PANDORA. Here, Reverend, under the trellis we'll be wed.

REVEREND. A beautiful spot.

PANDORA. Red roses grow all through the vines. After the ceremony everyone will throw scarlet petals in our path. Poor Mama's upset because the groom is late. She thinks he's not coming.

KANDALL. No, no, I'm sure he's coming. His son's arrived.

PANDORA. Which son?

KANDALL. Sidney.

PANDORA.   How wonderful! Ever since the divorce none of Edvard's children have spoken to him.

KANDALL. Please, I'd rather we didn't mention the scandal.

JONSEY. Yes, no.

PANDORA. Sssh! It's all a secret. *(Pause.)*

REVEREND. Lovely day.

KANDALL. Yes.

REVEREND. Gentle breeze. I see congratulations are in order.

FLORAL. What?

REVEREND.   *(To Floral and Jonsey.)* I see you're expecting. Congratulations.

FLORAL. Is it really that apparent? I'm carrying extremely small for my size. I really didn't realize my condition was noteworthy.

REVEREND. Forgive me.

JONSEY. No, no. We're very proud. Very pleased. We've hoped for this ever since the day we were wed.

FLORAL. Yes.

JONSEY. We had the perfect wedding.

FLORAL. Yes.

JONSEY. The day was perfect.

FLORAL. I was happy.

JONSEY. Everyone was transformed by our love. It was effortless.

PANDORA. I'm going to wear blue wings for my wedding.

REVEREND. Really? *(Everyone nods with dismal restraint.)*

PANDORA. Edvard once asked me what gift I would most like in all the world, and I told him, "Blue wings." He put it in his book that I said it. It's something I really said and he put it in his book. I am the girl in his book ... No one but Edvard has ever understood me.

KANDALL. Reverend, how was Nigeria?

REVEREND. Much squalor. Much sadness.

PANDORA. You're such a good man.

REVEREND. I'm afraid I'm not. I'm not. No, no. But I thank you for the thought.

PANDORA. You are good, really.

9

JONSEY. Very good in my book.

KANDALL. Let's go in and have refreshments.

JONSEY. Yes.

REVEREND. How nice.

JONSEY. Reverend, have you ever been married?

REVEREND. Yes, I mean no, no! *(Jonsey, Reverend, Kandall exit to the manor.)*

FLORAL. Pandora. Wait here a moment. I have something … Let them go. Let them get out of range.

PANDORA. What is it?

FLORAL. I love you.

PANDORA. Yes, I love you too.

FLORAL. I wanted you to know, in case you had any doubts. Having said that, I must ask you, why are you marrying this man?

PANDORA. He divorced his wife of twenty-three years and all of his children just for me.

FLORAL. Ask yourself ponderously, does that speak well of his character?

PANDORA. His character's not important. He's an artist.

FLORAL. So you have no doubts about your future? No gnawing concerns? I mean, the fact that he is over twice your age, myopic, rumored to be a drunkard, decidedly a philanderer, and has been known to wear a ponytail, makes no matter to you?

PANDORA. Not really, no.

FLORAL. Very well, as you wish.

PANDORA. Thank you, but you mustn't be concerned. He's everything I've ever wanted, all my heart desires, I couldn't be happier, if only he were more my age.

FLORAL. What can you do? He won't grow younger. I presume just older.

PANDORA. I wouldn't mind it, if only …

FLORAL. What?

PANDORA. His hands have spots.

FLORAL. Age spots, liver spots. Death spots.

PANDORA. Little brown ones. And there are grey hairs all over him. On his chest even. Another thing, he cries when he looks at me.

FLORAL. You're going to be his nursemaid.

PANDORA. I'm too young to be a nursemaid.

FLORAL. And yet it's your fate.

PANDORA. Oh, help me. You're my older sister. Please, save me. Make everything all right again. I'm too young for all this.

FLORAL. All right . I'll tell him. I'll break it off for you.

PANDORA. He's going to be so angry.

FLORAL. Then so he shall be … You must not sacrifice your life to some doddering relic, simply because he turned you into a silly legend.

PANDORA. I like being a legend.

FLORAL. But is it worth a bad marriage?

PANDORA. You have a bad marriage.

FLORAL. Why do you say that? Jonsey and I are very happy.

PANDORA. You seem to despise him. Yesterday you and I were going out to get malts, Jonsey asked to join us and you changed your mind immediately, saying you had no interest in a malt. When we returned with our malts, you cried, saying you had wanted one all along. Jonsey offered you his, but you shoved it away with such a force that it fell and splattered all over the cobblestones.

FLORAL. I suppose I simply did not want a malt after all. You don't understand being pregnant. There are cravings you cannot explain. These cravings are very deep and reason does not speak to them. Now shall I call off your wedding or not?

PANDORA. What do you think I should do?

FLORAL. Why ask me? It's your decision entirely. This will make or break your life and I won't be held responsible, only you can decide.

PANDORA. Ooh. Ooh. I don't know. Why ask me? Let's pull the petals off this flower. Whatever it says will be so. *(She picks a flower from the yard.)*

FLORAL. That is a childish way to make up your mind, a foolish solution.

PANDORA. I think it'd be fun to do it this way.

FLORAL. Fine. It's your life.

PANDORA. *(As she plucks petals from the flower.)* Yes, I'll marry; no, I'll not. Yes, I'll marry; no, I'll not. Yes, I will. No, I won't. Yes. No. Yes, no. Yes, no. It stopped.

FLORAL. Fine.

11

PANDORA. But my heart.

FLORAL. Too late. Live by the flower, die by the flower. The wedding is off. *(Kandall enters from the manor.)*

KANDALL. Refreshments are being served.

FLORAL. Mother, Pandora has something to tell you.

KANDALL. *(To Pandora.)* What?

FLORAL. There'll be no wedding.

KANDALL. Really?

PANDORA. Yes, she's right. She's right. He's repulsive. I never should have agreed to marry such a hairy old goat. After all, the flower would have told me the truth.

FLORAL. Nature doesn't lie.

KANDALL. There will be no marriage. The marriage is off.

PANDORA. What must we do?

KANDALL. Pick up the wedding cake immediately. I refuse to have the whole town viewing it as an emblem of our impetuous hearts.

PANDORA. I'll go with you. I want to see all the roses and swirls and turtle doves.

KANDALL. Are you very unhappy?

PANDORA. No. I'm very happy. Very, very happy indeed. *(Pandora and Kandall exit to the manor.)*

FLORAL. Well now, there's my good deed for the day. *(A beat as she breathes in the beauty of the garden.)* How it worries me. How it has me worried. *(Jonsey enters from the manor.)*

JONSEY. Ah, Floral! Mr. Edvard Lunt has finally arrived. Where's Pandora?

FLORAL. She's breaking off the engagement.

JONSEY. But, why?

FLORAL. Obvious reasons.

JONSEY. How shocking.

FLORAL. Bring him to me at once. I must explain the unfortunate situation.

JONSEY. Pandora's left it to you to break her engagement to this man?

FLORAL. An unpleasant chore. But I'll manage.

JONSEY. Did I tell you I love you today?

FLORAL. Yes.

JONSEY. Tonight I'll pour sweet oils for your bath and rub your belly and feet. My wife. My cherished mother-to-be.

FLORAL. Please bring him.

JONSEY. I love you, my love.

FLORAL. I love you, I love you, I love you too. *(Jonsey exits to the manor. She hums for a while, then speaks.)* All this waiting. *(Edvard Lunt, 50s, enters from the manor. He is an extremely appealing though decadent looking man.)*

EDVARD. Edvard Lunt. I've come in search of Pandora. I'm terribly late.

FLORAL. So lovely to meet you, Mr. Lunt. I'm Floral Whitman, Pandora's sister.

EDVARD. Yes, yes. You must forgive me. I was in a hotel fire. My cat was burnt. My documents destroyed. I thought of calling, but I would have missed the next flight and been even later.

FLORAL. Don't worry. It's never too late to do what's right. Don't you agree?

EDVARD. I do not. In fact, I believe we are defined by the things we can no longer feel, dream, or accomplish. The man who is no longer capable of scaling the mountain is quite different from the boy who has yet to try. Ah, indeed, if it were never too late to do anything, life would hold no meaning whatsoever.

FLORAL. Life hold no meaning. There are schools of thought which adhere to that philosophy.

EDVARD. A gravely unimaginative conclusion to these mysteries we behold. I adamantly reject the notion of meaningless existence.

FLORAL. Famous people generally do. Otherwise, the value of their fame would evaporate.

EDVARD. It's true, fame does help give meaning to life. In fact, fame helps a good deal.

FLORAL. On the other hand, I find it untragic that I have never done anything of use with my life. A big waste it has been. But that's not unusual. Most of us, most people are in that boat. It's a very full vessel. I'm afloat with a mob.

EDVARD. I don't know you. I can't say. You are having a child.

FLORAL. Another passenger on board.

EDVARD. You have a way of looking at things.

FLORAL. How kind you are and how polite. Did it ever occur to you my sister may be far too young for you?

EDVARD. No. I love her madly. What else matters?

FLORAL. That she comply. You'll forgive me for being rude, blunt and the bearer of bad news, when I tell you Pandora wants to call off the marriage. She feels it was a hasty decision, and now she has decided against it firmly.

EDVARD. Are you serious?

FLORAL. Quite.

EDVARD. Where is she? I must speak to her.

FLORAL. She never wants to see you again.

EDVARD. I can't. Please. Pandora! Pandora, my darling! Pandora! Where is she? Pandora! My life! My love! *(Pandora rushes in.)*

PANDORA. Edvard, my love! You've come! How I've missed you! How I feared you would never come!

EDVARD. Please don't toy with me. I can't. It's too awful. I'm too old.

PANDORA. Don't cry. Don't cry. You mustn't.

EDVARD. Your sister says you're having doubts about the wedding.

PANDORA. Just some jitters. Nothing of any matter. She doesn't know me. How can she tell what is in my heart? *(To Floral.)* Look how he's crying. Aren't you ashamed?

FLORAL. I have disgraced myself for you. I divorce you as my sister.

PANDORA. She's very jealous of me. What can I do? Everyone says I'm the beauty. And she's the plain one.

FLORAL. Ach!

PANDORA. Where have you been? Why are you so late?

EDVARD. I was in a hotel fire. My cat was burnt. My documents destroyed.

PANDORA. How I love the sound of your voice. Come, let me kiss off your tears. Such a wicked sister I have. *(They exit to the woods. Kandall enters.)*

KANDALL. She threw herself out of the moving car when she heard him shout her name.

FLORAL. Pity she didn't break her neck.

KANDALL. Please. We'll have to be happy for her now, when she gets married, and sad for her later, when she is married.

FLORAL. Divorce is an option.

KANDALL. People don't get divorced in our family. There's no

14

precedent. Besides, a divorce would be so vulgar.

FLORAL. Yes, true.

KANDALL. Oh, if only he'd die soon.

FLORAL. I must say, he looks even older in person.

KANDALL. Really? Oh my. *(Sidney enters.)*

SIDNEY. Good afternoon.

KANDALL. Hello, Sidney.

SIDNEY. I heard my father has arrived.

KANDALL. Yes, he has. What a lovely wedding it will be. We're all so thrilled.

SIDNEY. Marriage is an evilly antiquated institution. A suffocating environment where banality is bred.

KANDALL. So many opinions and yet so young.

SIDNEY. Indeed.

KANDALL. Tell me, Sidney, what of love? Do you regard love?

SIDNEY. Perhaps. Perhaps not. Love has yet to avail itself to my scrutiny.

KANDALL. There's been no one?

SIDNEY. In fact no. Not really. There was this one girl I liked. We would chat and talk about ice cream selection. She worked behind the counter and offered me unlimited free samples in small midget spoons. Often I couldn't make a decision, or up my mind, and would ask for her recommendation. Her preference. I would put it to her like this, "Which flavor would you get?" I always enjoyed whatever she selected or chose, until one day she picked Pistachio. I wasn't pleased with it. It wasn't up my alley. I told her this and she gave me a new cone. The Rocky Road. She took the Pistachio from me, threw it in a canister, and said I was not to pay her for it. I knew she couldn't be giving out free cones. I was aware the price of the second cone would be deducted from her small wages. So I left money for it. The cone. Too much money really, but I could not stand to wait for change. I never came back, of course, because it may have been an uncomfortable situation. Anyway, it could never have been the same.

FLORAL. This is a silly person.

SIDNEY. I didn't know you were listening.

FLORAL. I'm not a post! Mama, get a gun.

KANDALL. Let's go find your father so you can say, "Hello."

SIDNEY. Very well. Except he doesn't want to see me.

FLORAL. Please. Then why come?

SIDNEY. I have a message for him.

FLORAL. What message?

SIDNEY. A private message.

FLORAL. God, I would never have given you a free ice cream cone.

KANDALL. Please, Floral, try to be gracious. Let's go find your father. I'm sure he'll be delighted you've come.

FLORAL. I'll just stay here and pick at my wart.

KANDALL. Lovely. *(To Sidney.)* There are allowances you make for women in her condition. *(Sidney and Kandall exit to the manor.)*

FLORAL. *(About her stomach.)* My God. It's frightening. The growth. The undulations. *(The Reverend enters. He walks clumsily onto the scene.)*

REVEREND. Floral.

FLORAL. Reverend.

REVEREND. I ...

FLORAL. What?

REVEREND. I'm ... so happy for you.

FLORAL. And I for you.

REVEREND. Me?

FLORAL. A great trip you have had.

REVEREND. Something of a pilgrimage.

FLORAL. And all this time I have not missed you.

REVEREND. You've been very busy.

FLORAL. Not in the least. Nothing much has happened. Not a thing.

REVEREND. Your sister's marriage ...

FLORAL. I cannot be held responsible.

REVEREND. She professes deep love.

FLORAL. Meaningless protestations. Vaporous vows.

REVEREND. Sincerity is difficult to discern.

FLORAL. I'm in complete agreement.

REVEREND. It's kind of you to say.

FLORAL. I hope you don't mind, but I have so many things to do. *(Floral exits. Pandora and Edvard enter from the woods. Kandall, Sidney and Jonsey enter from the manor.)*

KANDALL. Floral, Jonsey says ...

16

PANDORA. Mother! He's here! Edvard, my beloved. He's come. I said he'd come, and he's come.

KANDALL. Mr. Lunt. What a great honor to make the acquaintance of a man of such global renown.

EDVARD. My pleasure entirely. I'm terribly sorry to be late.

KANDALL. Not at all. Everyone is just so thrilled about the wedding. And isn't it wonderful Sidney came all this way?

EDVARD. Sidney. Yes. So nice to meet you.

SIDNEY. We've met before.

EDVARD. Have we? Yes, of course. I remember the face very well. Where was it we met exactly? *(An awkward pause.)*

SIDNEY. My name is Sidney. I am your eldest son. You are my father.

EDVARD. Sidney? Oh no, no. You're far too old.

SIDNEY. Nevertheless, and be that as it may, I am Sidney Raymond Lunt, your eldest son.

EDVARD. Your voice has changed. Your face is different.

KANDALL. Perhaps he had a growth spurt.

EDVARD. Yes, at one time he was much younger. It's just there were so many offsprings. Eight altogether.

SIDNEY. Seven.

EDVARD. I exaggerate. It's my temperament. Well, I'm glad you've come after all. Very pleased indeed. I didn't think you children were speaking to me.

SIDNEY. We're not. I've come only to deliver something to you from Mother.

EDVARD. *(To Pandora.)* As long as it's not a poison cloak for Pandora. *(Laughs, then to Sidney.)* Well … what is it?

SIDNEY. I'd prefer to give it in private.

KANDALL. I'm off to pick up the cake. Pandora, Floral, please come assist.

JONSEY. Reverend, let me show you where the cardinals gather in the grove. *(Kandall and daughters exit. Jonsey and Reverend exit to the woods.)*

EDVARD. So you're Sidney, my son.

SIDNEY. Yes.

EDVARD. Amazing what time does.

SIDNEY. Yes.

EDVARD. Remember me reciting "Lament" to you?

SIDNEY. No.

EDVARD. I did for a while. Every night when we lived in Pittsburgh.

SIDNEY. We left Pittsburgh when I was two.

EDVARD. Is two too small to remember?

SIDNEY. I don't know. In any case, I don't.

EDVARD. Well, you should read it some time. It's an excellent poem.

SIDNEY. I'll look it up.

EDVARD. Do.

SIDNEY. Mother sent this note to you.

EDVARD. Thank you. *(Edvard takes the note, opens it; his eyes fill with tears.)* The way she writes, so small and blunt, workmanlike. No curlicues and with a pencil. This simple, terrible handwriting touches me to the heart. *(He returns the note to Sidney.)*

SIDNEY. Do you see what she says?

EDVARD. What does she say?

SIDNEY. She's going to kill herself if you marry Pandora. I'm to let her know as soon as the vows are exchanged, and she's throwing herself out the attic window.

EDVARD. She's not serious.

SIDNEY. She clawed her face with a nail. She'll do anything.

EDVARD. I cannot hear this.

SIDNEY. Please, do not force *M'amie* to jump from the attic. I could not live without her because of how I love her.

EDVARD. God.

SIDNEY. What are you thinking?

EDVARD. I wish you loved me the way you love her.

SIDNEY. You hardly ever lived with us. It's been years since we have spoken.

EDVARD. I don't know what to say to children.

SIDNEY. Of course, it's not your fault. Just please don't make my mother die.

EDVARD. I don't know what to do. A dark veil descends over the proceedings. If I call off the marriage, I'll be the victim of a coarse and scurrilous blackmail worthy of Pandora's eternal scorn. Yet if I marry, Margaret will kill herself. How could I live with her blood caked all over our marriage vows? What will I become? A coward? Or a killer? Oh God, this is an impossible way to start a marriage! Hand me that letter. I must see it once more. *(Sidney hands him the letter.)* How I am tormented by this measly handwriting. Don't tell Pandora. Tell no one. I must bear the burden alone.

SIDNEY. I'll bear it with you.

EDVARD. What can you do? You're no help. Go away from me with your glasses and beard. I pray I never grow as old as you. *(Edvard exits. Jonsey enters from the woods.)*

JONSEY. There were three cardinals in the grove. Bright red they were and in high spirits.

SIDNEY. I spoke with my father.

JONSEY. Nice to have a living father. My father's been dead for twenty-seven years.

SIDNEY. My father is a good man. Only he doesn't know what to say to children.

JONSEY. It was a boating accident. I watched him drown. You never really get over that shock. That shock of losing a parent. *(A beat. Lights fade to black.)*

PART TWO

Night. Pandora enters. She runs down the hill and begins dancing.

PANDORA. I'm dancing in the night. Everything's in bloom and I'm dancing in the night. All alone. Out here. Come look at me! Everyone, I'm dancing all alone out here in the night. I'm spinning under all of these stars and I can't stop! I will not stop. No one can ever make me stop. Never. Never … Where is my lover?

EDVARD'S VOICE. *(Offstage.)* I cannot see.

JONSEY'S VOICE. *(Offstage.)* We're coming! Don't trip! Mr. Lunt, watch yourself!

KANDALL'S VOICE. *(Offstage.)* Light the lantern. The

19

Reverend will bring candelabras. The light.

FLORAL'S VOICE. *(Offstage.)* I wonder if I got these warts out here touching frogs. *(Jonsey, Kandall, Floral, and Edvard enter from the manor. Jonsey carries a bottle of champagne. Kandall and Edvard carry champagne glasses. All have been drinking.)*

JONSEY. How lovely! What a vision you make!

PANDORA. Edvard, look at me. My hair has come unbound. Dance with me.

EDVARD. I do not feel the urge. I've just eaten too much.

JONSEY. I'll dance with you.

PANDORA. Ooh, Jonsey! *(Pandora and Jonsey dance beautifully together.)* Jonsey is the most wonderful dancer in the county. All the women seek his company. He's acclaimed.

KANDALL. Yes, everyone says he's a very good dancer.

FLORAL. And handsome. They all say it and it's true. My husband's a handsome man.

KANDALL. *(To Floral.)* Why don't you join in?

FLORAL. How can I? My feet are swollen. I can't be expected to twirl.

KANDALL. Why don't you rest? We'll get you a chair. Jonsey!

JONSEY. *Pardonnez-moi, Mademoiselle. (He rushes to Floral.)* There, dear. Let's remove these shoes. I'll massage your precious feet. *(Pandora continues dancing alone.)*

PANDORA. Look at me. I can't stop spinning! I can't stop spinning! *(She twirls herself into Edvard's arms.)* Hold me in your arms before I lose myself altogether. Wait. Wait. Where's the music? Wasn't there music playing? Violins. Harps. String instruments.

EDVARD. There's no music out here.

PANDORA. But I heard it all so clearly. Could it have been in my head? All in my head? How flustered I am with excitement. Tomorrow I will be wed. Tonight is the last night I stand on this planet a solitary person. I will never be alone again. Marriage is the most wonderful state. Never to be alone.

JONSEY. I've never been lonely a moment, since the day I said, "I do." Not one instant.

PANDORA. All of this love, it will last and last and last.

JONSEY. Yes.

EDVARD. Not necessarily. I mean my first marriage didn't last forever.

PANDORA. But it wasn't a good marriage.

EDVARD. For a time it was. In the end it fell apart. I met you.
(The Reverend and Sidney enter carrying candelabras.)

REVEREND. We've brought the candelabras. I found kind
assistance.

KANDALL. Ah, Sidney! Where have you been?

SIDNEY. I thought it best to keep my own counsel.

KANDALL. But you missed supper. Pheasant was served.

SIDNEY. I had a package of peanuts that was given to me on
the plane.

REVEREND. Where would you like the candelabras?

KANDALL. Over here. And there.

EDVARD. There's something terribly sad about the way this
evening is progressing.

PANDORA. What's sad? Tell me.

EDVARD. It's not something one can explain, but it is very sad
indeed. *(Edvard walks away from Pandora.)*

JONSEY. *(Rubbing oil into the palm of his hands.)* Now for the
primrose oil. A special blend all my own.

REVEREND. *(To Floral.)* Have you hurt your foot?

FLORAL. Not in the least. He does this regularly.

REVEREND. Oh.

SIDNEY. *(To Edvard, with great intensity.)* Have you given further
consideration?

EDVARD. Don't plague me. Enough! Enough. *(A moment of
silence. The golden light created by the candles is breathtaking.)*

KANDALL. Magnificent candelabras. The mood created.

PANDORA. I feel like the girl Edvard wrote about in his book.
Brimming with sadness and longing under flickering lights.

FLORAL. You mean Sandra in *The Zookeeper?*

PANDORA. Yes.

FLORAL. I suppose I'm not literary. Although I am a voracious
reader, psychologically astute, and a keen observer of human
behavior, still I don't see the likeness. The girl in the book, she has
a job. She feeds animals at the zoo.

PANDORA. Yes.

FLORAL. Well, Pandora, as most of us know, has never had a job of any sort. The only pets she ever had was a bowl of five unfortunate goldfish. The largest swiftly starved to death because she never fed them. When I pleaded with her to remove its rancid carcass, she refused, in a state of high hysteria. The remaining fish swiftly perished and the stench permeated our entire property. Only then was she finally forced by the household to flush the malodorous mess down the sewer.

PANDORA. I could not understand why I should throw out a fish because it was dead. It had done nothing wrong or unnatural, I still loved it. It was still my fish. Why should I toss it down the drain?

FLORAL. Because it stank.

EDVARD. Listen to her. Her heart is bigger than all of ours together. She teaches me so much. *(To Pandora.)* I thought my life was over, then I met you.

SIDNEY. What does this mean? Tell me, what are you saying?

EDVARD. She is my bride, for better or for worse.

SIDNEY. Is that your final answer?

EDVARD. Yes.

SIDNEY. Do you understand what this means?

EDVARD. Your mother makes her own decisions. I can't be held responsible.

SIDNEY. It's only because she loves you that she is killing herself.

PANDORA. Who's killing herself?

KANDALL. Let's have dessert.

EDVARD. My wife has threatened to jump to her death the instant our marriage vows are spoken.

PANDORA. Your marriage to me will kill her?

EDVARD. Only if she's crazy and only if she's told.

KANDALL. I do not like scandal. I will not invite it into my home.

EDVARD. Forgive me, I did not want the situation revealed. I knew it would cast a shadow. Yet it's unavoidable how truth seeps out of its hole and crawls toward the light.

KANDALL. It certainly is not unavoidable. I've never heard of such a thing.

PANDORA. *(To Edvard.)* How you must love me to go through with our marriage under such tragic duress.

SIDNEY. *(To Edvard.)* Just so you'll know. After *M'amie* kills

22

herself, I plan to take my own life with an unsharpened hatchet. I feel certain my fellow brothers and sisters will follow suit and do the same.

KANDALL. No, no. No, no, no. We cannot have a scandal of this magnitude in my garden. What a pity the wedding is called off.

PANDORA. Mama, please. Everything is prepared. It would break my heart. The whole town will whisper I've been jilted. Think of the shame.

KANDALL. Reverend, advise us swiftly. Give us your wisdom.

REVEREND. I have so little.

KANDALL. Don't dally with me. This is your vocation.

REVEREND. I believe you must seek to be with those you love and of whom you are beloved. *(Floral swoons, Jonsey attends to her.)*

SIDNEY. At any price? A whole family slaughtered?

REVEREND. To slaughter yourself in any sense is a sin. We must find love in our hearts, no matter how meager the supply.

SIDNEY. How grateful I am to have forsaken organized religion of any sort.

PANDORA. Mama, I want to have my wedding.

KANDALL. Let's wait a bit. We'll wait.

PANDORA. It's mid-May and everything's in bloom. I can't wait. Now is the time. If we must, we'll run off tonight and I'll never see or speak to you again. How I will miss you.

KANDALL. Pandora, don't do this to me.

PANDORA. Don't make me. I beg of you, do not make me.

KANDALL. Very well. The wedding will proceed as planned.

PANDORA. Yea!

SIDNEY. Then all must die. *(Sidney exits to the woods.)*

KANDALL. More champagne, please.

PANDORA. Thank you, Mama. We're going to be happier than anyone has ever been in all the world. Except perhaps for you and Daddy. My parents were very, very happy. Weren't you?

KANDALL. We were.

FLORAL. And Jonsey and I are very much in love. We're having a child together. Our first child. Tonight we'll pick a name. One for a boy and one for a girl.

JONSEY. Floral.

FLORAL. What?

23

JONSEY. To hear you speak of the child. Our child. You hardly ever do.

FLORAL. Why illuminate the obvious? Look at me. I'm gigantic! Elephantine even! Choo! Choo! Choo! Choo! Choo! Choo! *(She dances around like a comedic pig.)* I could accommodate a circus under this tent!

PANDORA. *(Laughing.)* I believe she could.

FLORAL. Three rings at least!

EDVARD. *(Overenthusiastic.)* Oh, I don't doubt your prowess in the slightest.

FLORAL. Nor should you. Nor should you!

REVEREND. Excuse me.

KANDALL. Reverend, where are you going?

REVEREND. Off.

PANDORA. What for?

REVEREND. To pray. *(Reverend exits to the manor.)*

PANDORA. He's such a very good man.

FLORAL. Everyone isn't always what they seem.

PANDORA. What do you mean?

FLORAL. Everything isn't always as pictured. Frankly, I'm carrying around a huge, empty frame with no walls to hang it on. A rectangle of steel. It weighs two thousand tons. My back aches, my shoulders burn, even though it's empty — the damn thing is heavy! As usual, no one knows what I'm talking about. They just wait for the noise to stop. I'm going to go roll down a hill. Can anyone understand that?

PANDORA. You're forgetting your shoes.

FLORAL. My feet will no longer fit in them. *(Floral exits to the woods.)*

KANDALL. Her moods swing, it's her condition. Our dessert is long overdue. Cherries jubilee. I'll retrieve it from the pantry.

PANDORA. Wait, Mama, I'll go with you. You'll need me.

KANDALL. What do you mean?

PANDORA. You'll see.

KANDALL. See? I don't want to see. I can't stand any more surprises ever again in my whole life. *(Pandora and Kandall exit to the manor.)*

JONSEY. A fine night.

EDVARD. Yes.

JONSEY. Glorious weather.

EDVARD. Umm.

JONSEY. I have been wondering, is it yours?

EDVARD. What?

JONSEY. The child Floral is carrying.

EDVARD. Excuse me?

JONSEY. I beg your pardon. My mind plays tricks. I'm a very handsome man.

EDVARD. Why would you make such a remark?

JONSEY. I don't mean to boast. It's simply true, don't you agree? I am handsome.

EDVARD. I suppose, yes, your face is well structured.

JONSEY. Regrettably, sex holds no interest to me. It doesn't even repulse me. I'm that flaccid, I'm afraid. But what makes it a tragedy, which is my point, is the fact that I am so very, very handsome.

EDVARD. I see.

JONSEY. I love Floral. I love her because she struggles so hard. But I have never had sex with her. Something is absent. That longing. I run her bath; massage her feet with oils; dab her wrists and neck with fine perfumes. I powder every crevice of her body and feel only calm. I flirt with other women to proliferate the myth that I am a cad. There are whispers about my prowess and endless adulteries. But nothing is ever revealed. There are no revelations to make. Nothing is hidden, all is illusion, misdirection and palming.

EDVARD. Whose child is it?

JONSEY. I don't know.

EDVARD. What does your wife say?

JONSEY. We pretend it's mine.

EDVARD. How?

JONSEY. I don't know, but we do.

EDVARD. That's very terrible.

JONSEY. I thought it was admirable.

EDVARD. It's chilling.

JONSEY. We're talking about the same thing. We mean the same thing. We're just using different words. I feel like a stroll, will you join me?

EDVARD. I'm very tired today. I was in a hotel fire. My cat was

25

burnt, my documents destroyed.

JONSEY. Well, certainly, you must get your rest. *(Jonsey exits to the woods. Kandall and Pandora enter from the manor with cherries jubilee.)*

KANDALL. If you had asked me, I would have said, "Impossible!" That I should live to see this day! A grown daughter of mine. *(To Edvard.)* Mr. Lunt, I'm mortified ... Floral has carved into your wedding cake.

PANDORA. She took a giant piece, leaving a lopsided mess.

KANDALL. I fear she must have eaten cake with her hands. Such grotesqueries. What have I raised?! God, what have I raised?!

EDVARD. But it really is a small matter.

KANDALL. Not if your mind works in metaphor! A deliberate desecration.

EDVARD. Are you certain it was Floral?

PANDORA. I saw her, after all, I watched her take it.

KANDALL. Did she? Did she eat it with her fingers?

PANDORA. Mother.

KANDALL. Tell me.

PANDORA. Yes.

KANDALL. My God.

PANDORA. And she has warts, Mother. She has warts on her fingers.

KANDALL. If this continues, we'll soon be searching for distant places in which she can be put out of our sight for long periods of time along with other criminals, lunatics and barbarians. I blame it all on Jonsey. She would not live in such a rageful state, if only he could be faithful.

PANDORA. Jonsey has not been faithful?!

KANDALL. You never heard me say that. It did not come from my lips! Erase! Erase!

PANDORA. I knew it all along. The whole town whispers.

KANDALL. *(Drinking more champagne.)* I hoped having a child would make a difference. And it has made him even more horribly attentive. Unfortunately, the more attentive he becomes, the more unbearable her behavior. It seems he cannot give her the one gift she craves, so all others are fruitless.

EDVARD. What gift does she crave?

26

KANDALL. Faithfulness.

EDVARD. How strange.

PANDORA. She went into counseling at the church. No one in our family had ever gone into counseling. There was no precedent. She had a session every week with the Reverend.

KANDALL. For a time she seemed happy.

PANDORA. Then he left for Nigeria.

KANDALL. Afterwards she became pregnant.

PANDORA. Or was it right before?

EDVARD. I'm very tired. Forgive me.

PANDORA. His cat was burnt earlier today.

KANDALL. How dreadful.

PANDORA. Won't you come in now, Mama?

KANDALL. No, no. I want to be out here and breathe some … air. Good night.

PANDORA and EDVARD. Good night. *(Pandora and Edvard exit to the manor.)*

KANDALL. A wedding. A wedding in my garden tomorrow with these people. Impossible. *(Sidney enters.)*

SIDNEY. Forgive me.

KANDALL. For what?

SIDNEY. For being in your line of vision.

KANDALL. Really, Sidney. Please don't be odd. Won't you come in with me and have some cherries jubilee.

SIDNEY. I beg you, stop treating me kindly. I am not here as a friend of these proceedings. I've come only to disrupt and annihilate.

KANDALL. In any case, you can still have jubilee.

SIDNEY. Forgive me, I cannot.

KANDALL. As you wish. You know, Sidney, we are not on opposite sides. I too would like nothing better than to see this engagement broken. Confidentially, I do not believe the match to be at all suitable. Champagne?

SIDNEY. I don't drink.

KANDALL. Why not?

SIDNEY. I like to keep a clear head.

KANDALL. What for?

SIDNEY. To deal with — the day — my business … I'm not clear on that.

27

KANDALL. Yes, I understand how confusing it often is — being rational.

SIDNEY. Mind-boggling really. Now that I hand it a thought. Pass it a glance. And so ... champagne, please. This could, after all, be my last night on earth. My last look at the moon.

KANDALL. Such a nice one.

SIDNEY. And stars.

KANDALL. Glittering; glittering; glittering. All in all, a fine last night. Cheers.

SIDNEY. Yes. *(They drink.)* Do you really think I'll be dead tomorrow?

KANDALL. Only if you have not a modicum of sense, and prove to be a completely ludicrous person.

SIDNEY. I understand your ridicule. But every time I shut my eyes I see ...

KANDALL. What?

SIDNEY. My mother's body falling. I could not live without my mother.

KANDALL. And yet you would.

SIDNEY. How would I?

KANDALL. You would breathe. You would breathe. *(Sidney breathes.)*

SIDNEY. Breathing helps.

KANDALL. Sidney, I want to tell you something.

SIDNEY. What?

KANDALL. A secret. Will you keep it?

SIDNEY. Yes.

KANDALL. I'm not well anymore.

SIDNEY. What?

KANDALL. Just that.

SIDNEY. You're ill?

KANDALL. Precisely.

SIDNEY. How ill?

KANDALL. Very much.

SIDNEY. Very much ill? I'm so sorry.

KANDALL. Fortunately, it's hopeless. There's more dignity that way, don't you agree?

SIDNEY. I don't understand. You look well.

KANDALL. Thank you. I make an effort.

SIDNEY. Have you told your daughters?

KANDALL. I feared it would cast a shadow.

SIDNEY. How can this be? I don't understand. You look so well. So very well. My heart has stopped. It ... stopped.

KANDALL. Breathe.

SIDNEY. I cannot.

KANDALL. Breathe. Breathe. Breathe. I've had a life. My husband's buried. Both daughters married. A grandchild on the way. That will have been enough of a life. What else is there to do? Endless travel? An old lady alone on a steamer, draped in wool, watching fog drift by, sipping tea. Remembering ... what? My first kiss. *(Sidney kisses her with passion.)* Good heavens.

SIDNEY. I love you.

KANDALL. You've kissed me on the lips. What in the world?

SIDNEY. Forgive me. I'm a young upstart, worthy only of contempt, to be thoroughly despised and roundly horsewhipped. *(He kicks down a row of toadstools.)*

KANDALL. Don't do that! You must stop! Foolish, stupid boy.

SIDNEY. What have I done?

KANDALL. You've destroyed the fairies' houses. Fairies live under toadstools. Tonight they will have no place to sleep. They will come home and be lost.

SIDNEY. No one ever told me about the fairies. No one ever came to take my teeth.

KANDALL. What a dreadful night this has turned out to be.

SIDNEY. I'm sorry I didn't know about them, the fairies. I would never have done it had I known. I have never meant to hurt anyone. *(Kandall exits to the manor. Sidney tries vainly to repair the fairy homes. Floral enters from the woods covered in dirt and grass and leaves. Her hair is wild.)* What has happened to you?

FLORAL. I've been rolling down hills. My heart has been dragged all through these woods, leaving a trail of red you can follow with your eyes closed because of the stench. *(Sidney exits in confused horror as the Reverend enters.)*

REVEREND. Floral, I'm so very grateful to have come upon you. I have some information to impart. Nothing noteworthy. In fact, a matter of no importance to anyone. I have come to the conclusion this evening that I must leave the church. It is not much, but it is all I have to sacrifice for my hypocrisy. I'm not a talented or impressive man. All I had to give the world was a few good deeds. I took the woman with no legs an Easter bonnet; I taught the blind child to sing; I allowed mosquitoes to suck my blood with impunity. All of this motivated by a desperate wish to have some value. And yet I betrayed it all. *(He looks away from her.)* The meaning of my life and the woman I esteem above all others. I beg her forgiveness. I do not expect it. In fact, I firmly believe forgiveness must never be granted. But I do crawl at your feet on my hands and knees now and always, and forever.

FLORAL. Please. Penitence is not necessary. Understand I am quite happy with my husband. We are having a family. All goes well. All is intact.

REVEREND. I'm relieved and joyous to know that your spirit survived the evil I perpetrated. You came to me for guidance and I carried you to iniquitous grounds.

FLORAL. Ridiculous man, I seduced you.

REVEREND. No, no, no. I seduced you.

FLORAL. You are quite incapable of seducing a harlot in Dante's inferno.

REVEREND. Oh, I am, I am, I most definitely am. I am not good at all.

FLORAL. You are good and you must not leave the church. Just as I must not leave my marriage.

REVEREND. No, you must not.

FLORAL. Why do you say that to me?

REVEREND. Because it is the right thing to say.

FLORAL. Is it? Is it?

REVEREND. Yes, it is.

FLORAL. Very well. *(A beat.)* Jonathan.

REVEREND. Yes, Floral?

FLORAL. Jonathan.

REVEREND. Floral …

FLORAL. I feel romance all in the air. It's ripping through me like flowers blooming through my skin.

REVEREND. I cannot bear this.

FLORAL. Do something.

30

REVEREND. You are another man's wife.

FLORAL. I was before.

REVEREND. And now with his child.

FLORAL. There it is. You think I'm unpleasantly large.

REVEREND. No, I think you're very pleasant in shape … Really quite … in total. Your shape, I find … My tongue has departed.

FLORAL. In bed you're so different.

REVEREND. I spark fires.

FLORAL. Yes.

REVEREND. It's all because of you. Only because of you. It would not be possible with anyone else.

FLORAL. Take me.

REVEREND. Where?

FLORAL. Wherever.

REVEREND. I have to go.

FLORAL. I will kill you.

REVEREND. Do. It would be a blessing.

FLORAL. How should I kill you?

REVEREND. However.

FLORAL. With my claws; my teeth; my body and soul.

REVEREND. Yes, yes, all that.

FLORAL. Until there is nothing. Nothing left but shreds, shreds, shreds.

REVEREND. I have to take you. There is no stopping me. No stopping this onerous affliction. *(He runs his fingers through her hair, pulls her head back, and kisses her neck.)* I can't. I can't. This is impossible. Impossible. *(He moves away from her.)*

FLORAL. Is it? Is it? Is it? I never cared for you at all. I am happily married. Happily, happily, happily. My child will come from a good home. Without any hint of scandal. *(To her child.)* And everything will be possible for you. My dear, my most secret dear. It will all be possible. *(Jonsey enters from the woods. He does not see the Reverend.)*

JONSEY. My God! I was looking for you.

FLORAL. I have been rolling down hills. Won't you bathe me, wash my hair, and soak me in fine scents? *(Floral grabs Jonsey in her arms. The Reverend exits to the woods.)* How I love you, my love. *(Floral kisses Jonsey desperately on the lips. They slowly pull apart and regard each other with profound sadness.)*

PART THREE

The following morning. Decor such as flowers, flowing lace, a harp have appeared, indicating the wedding is imminent. Kandall, dressed in a discreetly elegant mother-of-the-bride ensemble, stands dropping rose petals over the crushed toadstools. Floral enters from the manor in a flowing gown. She wears an ostentatious hat, huge earrings, a cumbersome necklace and bracelet. Throughout the Act these various accessories are removed.

FLORAL. Mother.

KANDALL. Oh my.

FLORAL. I read a book that suggested one emphasize accessories in the later stages of pregnancy. Is it too much?

KANDALL. It's perfect. For the occasion. *(She returns to dropping rose petals.)*

FLORAL. *(A beat.)* I'm sorry I lurched into the wedding cake. I was so hungry. I couldn't stop myself. There's no excuse. Just an overwhelming craving I could not control.

KANDALL. Forgive me, I thought we were civilized human beings, not animals. *(Kandall starts to exit.)*

FLORAL. Where are you going?

KANDALL. To get the show on the road. *(Sidney enters.)* Good morning, Sidney.

SIDNEY. Forgive me.

KANDALL. As you wish. *(Sidney and Kandall exchange a look. Kandall exits to the manor.)*

FLORAL. She can do so much with the tone of her voice. Why do you wear that awful beard?

SIDNEY. My fresh face is gruesome to me. Innocence repulses me on every level. I can't watch children playing in a school yard without experiencing revulsion.

FLORAL. Nevertheless you should shave.

32

SIDNEY. How can I? When under this growth is the despicable face of a pasty coward. After all this morning my father marries; my mother dies. That simple and I'm eating a muffin.

FLORAL. They are good, aren't they? May I have some?

SIDNEY. Yes. *(He gives her some of his muffin.)*

FLORAL. Now, in my opinion, if you were a man of character and truly loved your mother as you profess, you would not sit here impotently eating a muffin. You would take action.

SIDNEY. What should I do?

FLORAL. Stop him. Shoot him. Do something that would slow him down.

SIDNEY. Shoot my father?

FLORAL. To save your mother. If you don't have a pistol, I'll tell you, there's one in the kitchen hidden in the yellow sideboard, bottom left-hand drawer beside the silver trivets.

SIDNEY. All right . I'll go. It is my fate. *(Sidney exits to the manor. Floral remarks after him.)*

FLORAL. And bring more muffins! The ones with raspberries. How will it end? I see no end. No end. *(Edvard enters from the manor dressed as a groom. He is distracted and ill-at-ease. He carries his dress shoes and socks which he puts on in the following scene.)* Edvard Lunt.

EDVARD. Yes.

FLORAL. Last night there was a little misunderstanding between us that I must rectify. When I said there could be a circus performing under my skirt, I was implying — it was meant to be a joke. I was attempting to indicate, I was wearing a tent, a large, billowy dress. Because of the pregnancy I was so big and wearing such large garb, i.e., tents, that a circus could or would be capable of performing underneath. You (I assume) assumed I meant I could service a whole circus, I mean an entire company of clowns or whatever could come under my skirt with their lascivious little ladders and horns and party, party, party or whatever. Actually, it was a joke I could have phrased more carefully. Still your interpretation was not warranted.

EDVARD. In attempting to follow your amorphous train of thought, I seem to have derailed.

FLORAL. In any case, I'd like you to know I'm extraordinarily particular about who I see privately. I'm not a virgin, but other

33

than that, I am wholesome in the extreme. Having said that, I beg you to leave.

EDVARD. How can I leave? I'm to be married in three minutes.

FLORAL. You're in danger if you stay for this wedding.

EDVARD. Yes, yes. I have my doubts. I'm already suffocated by all of this ceremonial paraphernalia. When Margaret and I wed, it was simple. Everyone brought a dish and danced without shoes.

FLORAL. You could be shot.

EDVARD. No, no, in every sense I shall keep my shoes on and be civilized.

FLORAL. Being civilized is a rot.

EDVARD. I disagree. Without the tormenting friction between the civilized and the primitive, life would be bereft of its most rapturous flavor.

FLORAL. What flavor is that?

EDVARD. Erotic abandonment. For there is no eroticism in a wholly primitive world and no abandonment in a wholly civilized world.

FLORAL. Yes, yes, I see. Table manners are important. So that when we eat berries with our fingers and let the juices drip down our lips, a statement is made.

EDVARD. You have a way of looking at things.

FLORAL. How kind you are and how polite. Now to save your life rush immediately to the station, get on the first train that comes and go wherever it takes you.

EDVARD. Oh. To be free of all marriages forever. I will go. No, I love her. I cannot. And yet … *(Jonsey enters from the manor.)*

JONSEY. More drama. The Reverend was not to be found this morning. Servants went to search for him across the property and discovered him in a ditch. His clothes had to be laundered. Kandall was very cross.

EDVARD. What was he doing in a ditch?

JONSEY. Crying is what I heard. I'm holding the rings. I've Pandora's here. I'll hold yours as well.

EDVARD. Yes. I — I … It's not here. I did not bring it. I left it. I'll retrieve it at once. *(Edvard exits.)*

FLORAL. I don't believe he'll be back.

JONSEY. Nonsense. They're very much in love. And a beautiful wedding is just what we need today. *(Reverend enters.)* Good day, Reverend.

REVEREND. Mr. Whitman.

JONSEY. The groom went off, nervous nanny. He forgot his ring. An odd fellow. I believe he's European or his family was European or he's been to Europe. Excuse me, I'm such a torrential bore. I don't know how my wife puts up with me. I'm content with things going on and on the way they are. I never wanted an interesting life. I prefer a few familiar things: my estate; my yachts; my trusted staff and crew. *(Kandall enters.)*

KANDALL. We're ready to begin. This really should not take long. *(Indicating that Floral should begin the music.)* Floral, the harp.

FLORAL. Mama, not everyone is here.

JONSEY. The groom is absent.

KANDALL. You mean for good? *(Edvard enters with the ring.)*

EDVARD. It was in my pocket all along. But the wrong pocket. Not the one I thought.

JONSEY. Yes, naturally. Stand here. Hand me the ring. *(Floral plays beautiful music on the harp.)*

EDVARD. Has anyone seen my son, Sidney?

JONSEY. Shh. The bride. *(Pandora enters in a blue gown wearing blue diaphanous wings, and carrying a bouquet of blue and violet flowers. Everyone looks at her and reacts accordingly. Sidney enters silently. He watches a moment, then raises his pistol, pointing it at Edvard.)*

REVEREND. Dearly beloved …

SIDNEY. Stand back, all of you. I'm going to shoot my father. *(Everyone freezes.)*

KANDALL. Good heavens.

SIDNEY. There will be no marriage. The marriage is off.

EDVARD. My God, how mortifying. *(To Kandall.)* I'm terribly sorry.

SIDNEY. Everyone except my father will leave here at once.

FLORAL. Perhaps we should all go.

PANDORA. *(Running to Edvard.)* I won't leave you! Never, never!

EDVARD. Pandora, please.

SIDNEY. Get away from him. Stay away.

PANDORA. Write about how I died protecting you with my

35

blue wings.

SIDNEY. Don't be so sure I'll not blast those wings!

REVEREND. Hand me that gun, you ridiculous maniac. How dare you endanger these people?! *(The Reverend walks toward Sidney.)*

SIDNEY. Halt! Halt!

FLORAL. Halt!

REVEREND. Please, do you doubt for one instant I would not relish a bullet to the brain? Better yet, the heart. Blast it to shreds, all to shreds.

SIDNEY. You are mad. Be reasonable. I will shoot.

FLORAL. No!

KANDALL. Sidney, if you shoot that Reverend, I'll never speak to you again!

SIDNEY. Kandall, please don't say that! *(Sidney accidentally shoots his own foot. He falls to the ground. everyone is aghast.)*

FLORAL. My God, he's been shot.

KANDALL. Yes, he has.

SIDNEY. I'm such a failure, a failure, an abject failure.

PANDORA. You saved us, Reverend. You're such a very good man.

SIDNEY. I don't know what to do. I'm bleeding. Help me. Reverend, help.

REVEREND. Don't ask me for help. I'm through giving help. Here, take this collar. Have it. It's more fit for a beast than a man. I'm sick from answering prayers and doing good deeds. It has turned me into a raving lunatic and left me with desperate, unquenchable desires. I want to spit on all altars for the remainder of my days. God, I am wretched. *(He exits to the woods.)*

SIDNEY. Someone, help me.

PANDORA. You got what you deserved.

SIDNEY. I cannot bear the sight of blood.

KANDALL. Mercy, mercy. Take him back to the manor, our house physician must tend his wounds. *(Jonsey and Edvard go to lift Sidney. Sidney winces in pain.)*

SIDNEY. Oh Father. Father.

EDVARD. There, there. *(Reciting from Dylan Thomas' "Lament".)*
    "'When I was a windy boy and a bit
    And the black spit of the chapel fold

(Sighed the old ramrod, …'"
SIDNEY.
"'… dying of women) …'"
SIDNEY and EDVARD.
"'… I tiptoed shy in the gooseberry wood … The rude owl cried like a telltale tit …'"*

(Pandora, Jonsey, Sidney, Edvard exit to the manor.)

KANDALL. Amazing. It all has gone off so much worse than expected.

FLORAL. A surprising turn of events.

KANDALL. Yes. And I wonder, Floral, how Sidney came across my grandfather's silver pistol?

FLORAL. I confess …

KANDALL. What?

FLORAL. I confess I did not want things to go off smoothly; so I orchestrated a few bumps.

KANDALL. You wicked thing! To do this to your sister.

FLORAL. She'll be grateful. After all, marriage isn't for everyone. Once you are married you're stuck. Nothing ever changes. Every year there's a turkey at Thanksgiving and a goose at Christmas. Jonsey gives me one more letter opener for my collection and no one ever sends me any mail.

KANDALL. Tradition cements our sanity.

FLORAL. But if I wanted things to be different, would it all crumble?

KANDALL. Are you saying you want a goose for Thanksgiving?

FLORAL. I'm saying this is not Jonsey's child.

KANDALL. Dear. Dear, dear, dear, dear, dear.

FLORAL. What shall I do?

KANDALL. Don't tell Jonsey.

FLORAL. I haven't.

KANDALL. Good.

FLORAL. But I suspect he knows.

KANDALL. How?

FLORAL. We don't have sex.

KANDALL. Since when?

FLORAL. Ever.

*From "The Lament" by Dylan Thomas. Copyright 1937 by Dylan Thomas

KANDALL. Oh dear, dear, dear, dear, dear, dear. What does he say?

FLORAL. He says I'll make a wonderful mother. That all along he has wanted a child and we'll have a beautiful happiness … Something. I don't know.

KANDALL. This is all good.

FLORAL. I don't love him.

KANDALL. Of course. I see. You have a lover.

FLORAL. No.

KANDALL. But you did.

FLORAL. That one.

KANDALL. What does he say about the child?

FLORAL. I haven't told him it is his. He assumes it's Jonsey's.

KANDALL. This is really quite a mess. And on the day of your sister's wedding. It reminds me of when you got that horrid green gum stuck in your hair on Confirmation Day. Well, we can't cut this out with scissors and cover it with a wide-brimmed hat.

FLORAL. *(Weeping.)* No.

KANDALL. Don't cry. Well, do if it helps.

FLORAL. Nothing helps. You see, all along all I have wanted was to emulate you and Father. How you loved each other.

KANDALL. We didn't love each other.

FLORAL. You always said you did.

KANDALL. Yes, because we didn't want you children to know how much we suffered. You might have gotten the wrong idea about marriage.

FLORAL. We might have gotten it all wrong.

KANDALL. I couldn't let that happen.

FLORAL. No, no. I love you, Mama.

KANDALL. I love you too.

FLORAL. Tell me what to do.

KANDALL. Think of it like this. Eventually, we'll all be dead. Your travails will have ended and you can rest in peace, knowing you have experienced the pain, confusion, and various con-tretemps that give life girth.

FLORAL. But what about the scandal?

KANDALL. It shall be monumental. All will be raked over coals and publicly crucified without mercy.

FLORAL. I'm so sorry.

KANDALL. Oh, after all, who gives a damn? *(They embrace. Pandora enters from the manor. She wears her wings over her honeymoon suit.)*

PANDORA. Mother, Edvard and I have decided not to be bullied and blackmailed by his deranged ex-spouse. We're driving over to Lordsley County, where we will be wed at once by the Justice of the Peace who awaits our arrival.

KANDALL. Darling, you are determined.

PANDORA. Yes, quite. And please do not suspect it is because I am in her woeful condition. I've no intention of ever having children. What they can do to you.

KANDALL. Yes, I know. I'm aware. How's Sidney?

PANDORA. A scratch, a flesh wound, nothing of note. He turned out to be entirely unremarkable. *(Kandall takes a breath of relief.)*

KANDALL. I'll go in and wrap up the top tier of your wedding cake for you to take.

PANDORA. Thank you, Mama. Oh, isn't this romantic! We're running off to be wed outside the arms of the church.

KANDALL. Also some rose petals and champagne. *(She exits to the manor.)*

PANDORA. Yes, yes, yes, yes, yes, yes! What do you imagine happened to the Reverend? Such scandalous behavior.

FLORAL. Pandora.

PANDORA. Good-bye, Floral.

FLORAL. I love you.

PANDORA. I love you too.

FLORAL. Having said that, I must tell you, I am very jealous of you.

PANDORA. Of course you are.

FLORAL. I've plotted against your wedding.

PANDORA. I know you have.

FLORAL. My marriage is a morbid predicament without passion or hope. You have such brave gaiety, romantic notions, youthful daring and translucent beauty.

PANDORA. Yes, but there's a terror to it.

FLORAL. What terror?

PANDORA. I play the lovely, joyous child everyone adores and is drawn to, but sooner than later my face will be less round, my eyes will dull, worry lines will cross my hardened brow, and I will become something that once was and now is not. My charms will not age well. Now is my time. I must take it. *(Edvard and Jonsey enter from the manor.)*

EDVARD. My beloved.

JONSEY. Your car awaits.

PANDORA. Yes. I'll gather my fallen bouquet. Oh, beautiful blue flowers, blue … *(Throughout the following, Pandora picks up her flowers, smells them and twirls.)*

EDVARD. Look at her. So pleased with the newness of the day. A brand-new penny that has not been dropped down toll booths, handed to beggars, thrown into wishing wells, flipped for bets or used in bad magic tricks.

PANDORA. Jonsey, dance!

JONSEY. Mademoiselle! *(Pandora and Jonsey dance.)*

EDVARD. And yet I have my doubts.

FLORAL. Who doesn't?

EDVARD. Many don't.

FLORAL. Hated multitudes.

JONSEY. *(To Pandora.)* Oh, your rings! I'm holding your rings!

PANDORA. Give me! Give me! *(Jonsey gives Pandora the rings.)*

EDVARD. Pestilence and hope were in Pandora's box. Hope was the salvation. Or was it the final pestilence?

FLORAL. An argument for the ages.

JONSEY. What are they talking about?

PANDORA. Nonsense. Good-bye Jonsey. Our rings. Don't lose. *(Pandora gives Edvard the rings.)* Good-bye, dear sister.

JONSEY. My most heartfelt congratulations to you both.

FLORAL. Pandora.

EDVARD. Farewell, all of you! Farewell. Auf Wiedersehen. *(Pandora and Edvard exit to the manor.)*

JONSEY. An odd man. He thought jasmine were honeysuckle.

FLORAL. I want to ask you a question.

JONSEY. Naturally, I wish them well and hope they have a most pleasant life. People deserve such things.

FLORAL. Your lovers? Which ones have been your lovers?

JONSEY. Floral. How strange.

FLORAL. Everyone knows about your infidelities. I've known for some time. I suspect even my mother suspects.

JONSEY. But I don't have lovers. Darling, you, of all people, must know. You know I cannot ... It's quite clear I cannot.

FLORAL. With me.

JONSEY. With everyone.

FLORAL. I thought only me. You flirt with so many.

JONSEY. So they won't know. So you won't be ashamed.

FLORAL. My. You see, all along I thought it was only me.

JONSEY. I beg your pardon. I thought it was all apparent. I assumed you knew that my attention to others was merely a guise to make us appear normal.

FLORAL. No. I missed that.

JONSEY. Now you understand.

FLORAL. Yes.

JONSEY. Good.

FLORAL. I think I have to leave you.

JONSEY. No. Impossible. You're my wife. That's my child.

FLORAL. It's not.

JONSEY. We'll say it is. I'll love it like it is.

FLORAL. Love can't make it so.

JONSEY. What can?

FLORAL. It has to be.

JONSEY. I see. I see. There's nothing I can do.

FLORAL. About what?

JONSEY. Anything. Everything. I give up. I surrender. Wrap me in a white flag and ship me towards death. Better than whining and wanting like an undignified dog. Don't you agree?

FLORAL. Well, I do believe it has been your character.

JONSEY. Best not be without character.

FLORAL. People can change.

JONSEY. Who told you that? They were lying.

FLORAL. I've seen it happen.

JONSEY. Well, best believe your own eyes.

FLORAL. (A beat.) What are you thinking?

JONSEY. I'm trying to recall if you said anything clever yesterday. Something I could compliment you on today.

FLORAL. Ah.

JONSEY. So rarely do I look people in the eye and wonder what

41

they are thinking. What if it were something that could spoil the day? Because what you are thinking is exactly the opposite of what I am thinking. It's diametrically opposed. That's not to say I believe you to be wrong and me to be right or vice versa. Truthfully, my belief system is lenient to a grave degree. There is no point at which my spine is not wholly gelatinized. And yet I'm so handsome. *(Sidney enters from the manor. His foot is bandaged and he limps with his cane.)*
SIDNEY. Hello.
JONSEY. Sidney Lunt. I was just explaining to Floral why it is that we have such a very bad marriage. You see, she snores. I've never really been able to abide it, that trait. I've kept it to myself all these years, but it is something that has disturbed me every night of my life and I can no longer keep quiet about it. This is not to say, dearest wife, that I do not adore you in many other respects. However, this grievance strikes a chord so deadly deep that I must insist we seek a divorce at once. Don't you agree?
FLORAL. Yes, I agree.
JONSEY. Very good. You are our witness, Sidney. Good day. *(Jonsey exits.)*
SIDNEY. I have your muffin.
FLORAL. Yes. *(Sidney offers Floral the muffin. She takes it.)* Sidney, in retrospect, I must say the gun suggestion was a mistake.
SIDNEY. No question. No question. However, I was able to call M'amie and report that the wedding did not take place. She was quite happy. For the moment.
FLORAL. Hope. *(The Reverend enters from the woods.)*
REVEREND. Hello, Sidney. Floral.
FLORAL. What has happened to you?
REVEREND. I have been rolling down hills and giving vigorous thought to the question ... The question: what is impossible? The answer is, a formidable lot. To dance from here to the stars; to eat a tribe of bees; to scream down a forest; to remember when you were born; to know when you will die; to stop breathing and live. Many things are impossible. Endless things are impossible. Our life together is not quite that.
FLORAL. Not impossible?
REVEREND. Tricky, yes.

FLORAL. Jonathan. I must ... Must I? Must I speak the truth? Oh. I feel as though I'm going to perish. If only I would perish.
REVEREND. Don't perish. Please. No.
FLORAL. This is your child I am carrying. I am in love with you. I want to be with you forever.
REVEREND. Impossible.
FLORAL. What will happen to us?
REVEREND. Many things. But not in this garden.
FLORAL. Where?
REVEREND. *(Touching his heart, her heart; then taking her hand and leading her out of the garden.)* Here. Here. Here. *(Gesturing to the whole world.)* Here. *(They exit to the woods. Offstage.)* Here. *(Kandall enters. She holds raspberries in her hands and eats them with her fingers.)*
KANDALL. Sidney, you have made a shambles of the day.
SIDNEY. I've behaved abominably. There's no doubt.
KANDALL. My children. My girls. Their little lives are just ruined.
SIDNEY. Things do not look promising. Floral has departed with the Reverend.
KANDALL. To seek counsel?
SIDNEY. No. It seems ... Apparently ... If I am not wholly mistaken ... He is the father of her child.
KANDALL. *(Taken aback.)* Oh. I missed that. Is it too late for me to change?
SIDNEY. What would you change?
KANDALL. I would change my life.
SIDNEY. Yes, it's too late to change that.
KANDALL. The rest of it though. All the rest could be different.
SIDNEY. I believe so.
KANDALL. Kiss me, Sidney. *(A silence. He cannot.)*
SIDNEY. *(Taking her hand.)* Forgive me.
KANDALL. For what?
SIDNEY. You see I am such an impossible fool.
KANDALL. Oh, I understand. I remember my first kiss. Far away in the garden under the arbor. I was seven and the boy was nine. He grabbed me by the puffs of my sleeves and pulled me to him. We kissed full on the mouth, I was terrified and ran away. Afterwards I felt wicked and was in a mood for days. At night, in

43

bed, I'd remember the dark secret. My heart pounding my body trembling. How it was all so quick and slow.
SIDNEY. May I trouble you for one raspberry before I go?
KANDALL. Of course. I have plenty. *(She offers the berries to him. He carefully takes one and slips it into his mouth.)*
SIDNEY. Mmm.
KANDALL. Yes.
SIDNEY. *(Not going.)* I'm off.
KANDALL. *(Offering him berries.)* It was lovely to have met.
SIDNEY. And so ...
KANDALL. Yes. *(They stay eating berries together. FADE TO BLACK.)*

END OF PLAY

PROPERTY LIST

Cane (SIDNEY)
Handkerchief (FLORAL)
Chocolate (JONSEY)
Note (SIDNEY)
Cherries jubilee (KANDALL, PANDORA)
Rose petals (KANDALL)
Muffin (SIDNEY)
Shoes and socks (EDVARD)
Ring (EDVARD)
Harp (FLORAL)
Bouquet of flowers (PANDORA)
Pistol (SIDNEY)
Rings (JONSEY)
Raspberries (KANDALL)

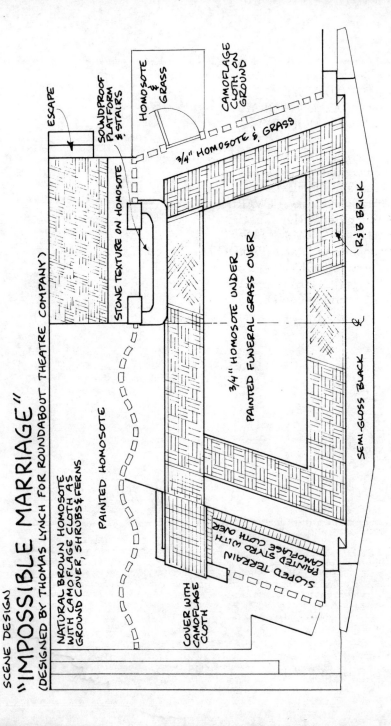

SCENE DESIGN

"IMPOSSIBLE MARRIAGE"

(DESIGNED BY THOMAS LYNCH FOR ROUNDABOUT THEATRE COMPANY)

ESCAPE

SOUNDPROOF PLATFORM & STAIRS

HOMOSOTE & GRASS

CAMOFLAGE CLOTH ON GROUND

3/4" HOMOSOTE & GRASS

STONE TEXTURE ON HOMOSOTE

R & B BRICK

3/4" HOMOSOTE UNDER PAINTED FUNERAL GRASS OVER

SEMI-GLOSS BLACK

NATURAL BROWN HOMOSOTE WITH CAMOFLAGE CLOTH AS GROUND COVER, SHRUBS & FERNS

PAINTED HOMOSOTE

SLOPED TERRAIN PAINTED STYRO WITH CAMOFLAGE CLOTH OVER

COVER WITH CAMOFLAGE CLOTH